Published in 2014 by The Rosen Publishing Group, Inc.
29 East 21st Street, New York, NY 10010

Photo Credits: **KEY** tl=top left; tc=top center; tr=top right; cl=center left; c=center; cr=center right; bl=bottom left; bc=bottom center; br=bottom right; bg=background

DT = Dreamstime; GI = Getty Images; iS = istockphoto.com; SH = Shutterstock; TF = Topfoto; TPL = photolibrary.com

front cover c, bg SH; **back cover** bc TPL **10**tr iS; bl, bg SH; br TF; **11**br iS; cr, cr, tl, tr, bg SH; **12**tr iS; **13**c TPL; **17**tr, cr iS; br SH; **18**c, c SH; **20**cl iS; bc, c, c, cl SH; bl TPL; **20–21**tc, bc iS; **21**tc, bc iS; **22**cr GI; c SH; **25**br iS; **27**c GI; bc iS; c, c SH; bc TPL; **28**bc, bg SH; cr TF; **29**bl DT; tr SH; **30**bg SH; **31**bg SH

All illustrations copyright Weldon Owen Pty Ltd

Weldon Owen Pty Ltd
Managing Director: Kay Scarlett
Creative Director: Sue Burk
Publisher: Helen Bateman
Senior Vice-President, International Sales: Stuart Laurence
Vice President Sales North America: Ellen Towell
Administration Manager, International Sales: Kristine Ravn

Library of Congress Cataloging-in-Publication Data

McFadzean, Lesley.
 Forest habitats / by Lesley McFadzean.
     pages cm. — (Discovery education: Habitats)
 Includes index.
 ISBN 978-1-4777-1326-6 (library binding) — ISBN 978-1-4777-1487-4 (paperback) — ISBN 978-1-4777-1488-1 (6-pack)
 1. Forest ecology—Juvenile literature. I. Title.
 QH541.5.F6M44 2014
 577.3—dc23
                            2012043671

Manufactured in the United States of America

CPSIA Compliance Information: Batch #S13PK3: For Further Information contact Rosen Publishing, New York, New York at 1-800-237-9932

Discovery
EDUCATION™

FOREST HABITATS

LESLEY MCFADZEAN

PowerKiDS
press™
New York

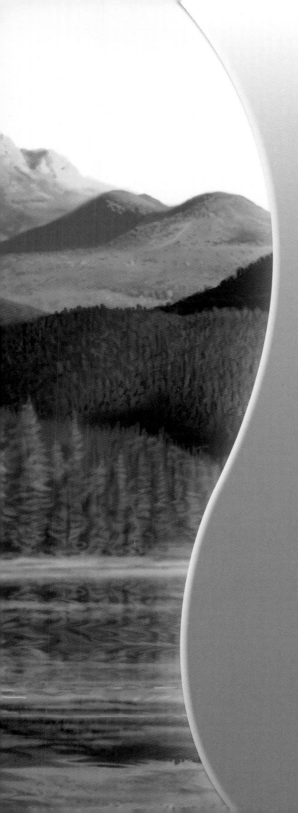

Contents

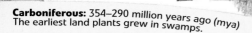

Carboniferous: 354–290 million years ago (mya)
The earliest land plants grew in swamps.

Permian: 290–248 mya
Seed-bearing trees evolved in the cool Permian.

Triassic: 248–206 mya
Cycads flourished in the drier

Trees: Past and Present

For millions of years after the Big Bang, Earth was a hot, gas-filled, lifeless planet. It was only 400 million years ago that the first true land plants appeared. From these ancient ancestors, today's spore-bearing trees, then seed-bearing and, finally, flowering trees evolved.

Gingko
Only one species remains of this group of Permian seed-bearing trees, called gymnosperms.

Cycads
Cycads, with large seed-bearing cones, emerged in the Triassic and 140 species survive today.

Conifers
Conifers are the most common gymnosperms —550 species have survived or evolved since the Jurassic.

Horsetails
Horsetails, which reproduce from dusty specks called spores, still resemble their Carboniferous ancestors.

Red–flowering gum
The most advanced angiosperms dominate the world of trees today.

Magnolia
A primitive flowering tree, or angiosperm, magnolia evolved in the Cretaceous.

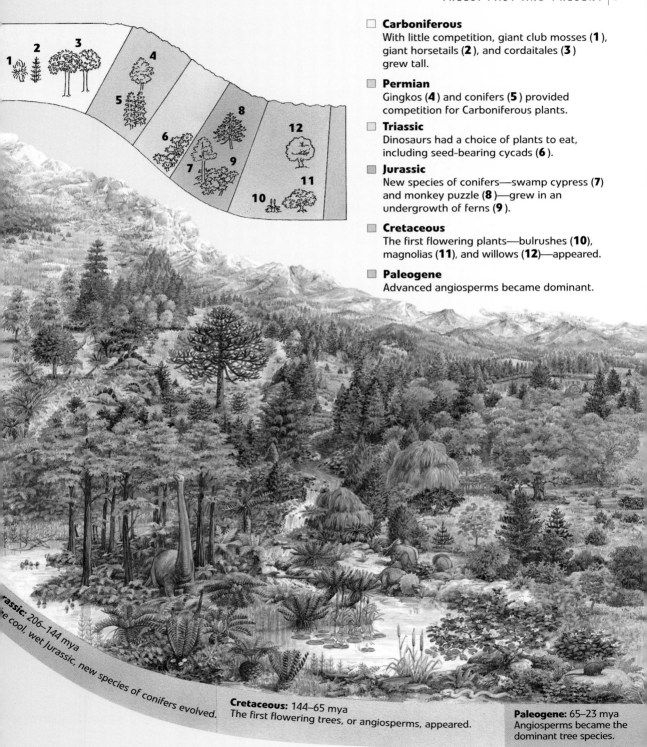

☐ **Carboniferous**
With little competition, giant club mosses (**1**), giant horsetails (**2**), and cordaitales (**3**) grew tall.

☐ **Permian**
Gingkos (**4**) and conifers (**5**) provided competition for Carboniferous plants.

☐ **Triassic**
Dinosaurs had a choice of plants to eat, including seed-bearing cycads (**6**).

☐ **Jurassic**
New species of conifers—swamp cypress (**7**) and monkey puzzle (**8**)—grew in an undergrowth of ferns (**9**).

☐ **Cretaceous**
The first flowering plants—bulrushes (**10**), magnolias (**11**), and willows (**12**)—appeared.

☐ **Paleogene**
Advanced angiosperms became dominant.

rassic: 206–144 mya
e cool, wet Jurassic, new species of conifers evolved.

Cretaceous: 144–65 mya
The first flowering trees, or angiosperms, appeared.

Paleogene: 65–23 mya
Angiosperms became the dominant tree species.

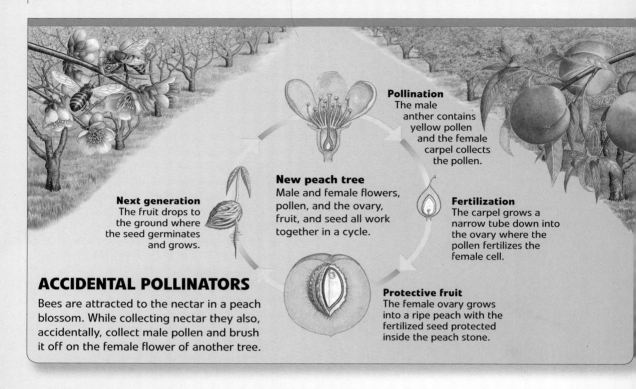

Pollination
The male anther contains yellow pollen and the female carpel collects the pollen.

New peach tree
Male and female flowers, pollen, and the ovary, fruit, and seed all work together in a cycle.

Next generation
The fruit drops to the ground where the seed germinates and grows.

Fertilization
The carpel grows a narrow tube down into the ovary where the pollen fertilizes the female cell.

Protective fruit
The female ovary grows into a ripe peach with the fertilized seed protected inside the peach stone.

ACCIDENTAL POLLINATORS

Bees are attracted to the nectar in a peach blossom. While collecting nectar they also, accidentally, collect male pollen and brush it off on the female flower of another tree.

Germination and Growth

Trees are rooted to one spot and need help to produce the next generation. Insects, birds, mammals, and the wind carry male pollen to trees with mature female cells. After the seed has been pollinated, an embryo starts to grow inside it. A seed needs light, warmth, and moisture to sprout its first stem and root—a process called germination. If the seed drops beneath the parent tree, the large tree will compete with the tiny seed for sunlight and water. Papery wings allow the wind to transport some seeds, while others rely on animals eating then passing the undigested seed in what could be the ideal spot.

Land at last
Coconuts, though heavy, are built to float and can travel thousands of miles before being washed ashore.

Floating coconuts

Coconuts are far too large to be blown by the wind or swallowed by an animal. Coconut trees depend on oceans and rivers to transport their seeds. The seed floats and is eventually washed onto a sandy beach or riverbank.

That's Amazing!

Eucalyptus trees rely on fire to explode seed casings and scatter their seeds. The parent trees may burn, but they leave space for the new seeds to germinate in the burned forest.

Ready to sprout
With energy from its own food supply—coconut milk—the embryo sends out its first stem and root.

Breaking open
The roots gather moisture from the ground and the shoots grow strong enough to break open the coconut.

Roots and Bark

Every part of a tree has its role or roles. Tree roots not only provide a solid foundation to support the weight of the tree but also collect the water and minerals from the soil that the tree needs to survive. The role of the bark is to protect the growing wood in the tree trunk. The bark itself is made up of dead cells but, by keeping pests out and moisture in, the bark protects the living cells in the layers beneath it.

Mangrove roots
Mangroves, which grow in shallow water, have stilt roots that anchor the tree and absorb oxygen from the air.

Buttress roots
Rain forest trees have shallow roots. Additional roots above the ground are needed to support, or buttress, tall trees.

Banyan roots
The spreading branches of banyan trees need additional support. Aerial roots grow down from the branches to form extra trunks.

Spring growth spurt

Late summer growth

Growth rings

Some trees have growth spurts in spring and early summer, grow less in late summer, and stop growing in the fall and winter. In a cross-section, the light-colored rings show growth spurts over spring; the dark-colored rings show late summer growth.

Layer upon layer

The four outer layers of a tree trunk contain different types of cells that protect, produce new bark, carry nutrients from the leaves to the rest of the tree, or promote growth. Underneath these layers are the sapwood and the heartwood, or core, of the trunk.

Damaged bark

When there are no berries or nuts available, squirrels chew through the bark of trees to reach the sweet sap beneath. The damage they cause takes time to repair itself.

Sapwood

Heartwood

Bark contains dead cells.

Cork cambium contains new cells.

Phloem carries nutrients from the leaves.

Vascular cambium contains growth cells.

Distinctive barks

It is not only leaves that help us to identify trees. Some trees have such distinctive bark that this alone can tell us the species.

Rainbow eucalyptus

Plane tree

Pine tree oozing sap

Black walnut

Photosynthesis

E very living thing needs energy to live and grow. Animals hunt and gather the food that provides their energy, but this option is not available to trees. Instead, trees manufacture their own nutrients in a process called photosynthesis. A combination of carbon dioxide (CO_2), water (H_2O), and minerals is stored in the leaves. When the sun comes up and shines on the leaves, a chemical reaction combines the raw ingredients into glucose, which moves to all parts of the tree.

Sunlight
Leaves act like solar panels to absorb sunlight, which provides the energy for photosynthesis.

Cleaning the air
In forests of growing trees, photosynthesis cleans the atmosphere by taking in significant quantities of carbon dioxide (CO_2) and expelling oxygen (O_2).

Rain falls and some evaporates.

H_2O

Oxygen (O_2) is released into the atmosphere.

O_2

Carbon dioxide (CO_2) is absorbed.

CO_2

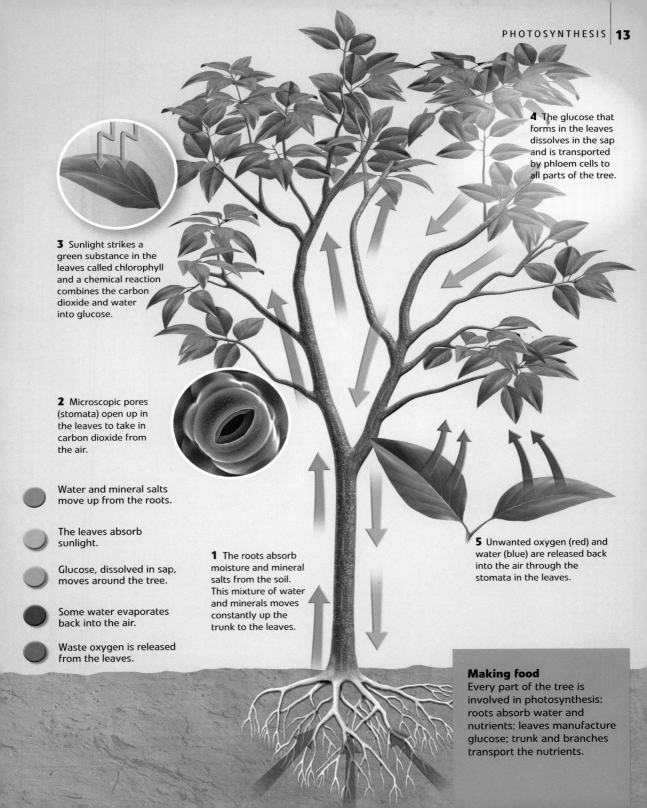

4 The glucose that forms in the leaves dissolves in the sap and is transported by phloem cells to all parts of the tree.

3 Sunlight strikes a green substance in the leaves called chlorophyll and a chemical reaction combines the carbon dioxide and water into glucose.

2 Microscopic pores (stomata) open up in the leaves to take in carbon dioxide from the air.

Water and mineral salts move up from the roots.

The leaves absorb sunlight.

Glucose, dissolved in sap, moves around the tree.

Some water evaporates back into the air.

Waste oxygen is released from the leaves.

1 The roots absorb moisture and mineral salts from the soil. This mixture of water and minerals moves constantly up the trunk to the leaves.

5 Unwanted oxygen (red) and water (blue) are released back into the air through the stomata in the leaves.

Making food
Every part of the tree is involved in photosynthesis: roots absorb water and nutrients; leaves manufacture glucose; trunk and branches transport the nutrients.

Identifying Trees

Gymnosperms have needle-shaped leaves, seeds inside cones, and are evergreen. Angiosperms have broad leaves, flower each year, grow seeds inside fruits, and many are deciduous (shed their leaves in fall). There are thousands of species in each group and a tree's shape, bark patterns, leaves, cones, flowers, and fruits are used to identify species.

Moreton Bay fig
This large, spreading rain forest tree has buttress roots. Its figs are initially orange in color but purple when ripe.

American elm
The broad-topped American elm has fruits that are flat, with papery wings around the seeds that allow them to fly.

English oak
The majestic English oak is deciduous. Its acorns are long, with a cup at the base that covers up to one-third of the nut.

Silver birch
The silver birch has long male and female flower spikes called catkins. The leaves are triangular, with pointed tips and serrated edges.

Sugar maple
The sugar maple leaf, which appears on Canada's flag, has three large and two small lobes. It has a double-winged seed.

Common beech
The fruits of the deciduous common beech are triangular nuts that grow, usually in pairs, inside a spiky covering.

Monterey pine
A Monterey pine has a rounded top, long, blunt-tipped needles that grow in clusters, and egg-shaped cones.

Balsam fir
The slow-growing balsam fir with its pointed top has flat needles and large cones that stand upright on the branches.

Atlas cedar
This pyramid-shaped coniferous tree has needles that grow in a whorl. Its cylindrical cones are flat topped.

Coast she–oak
She-oaks have what look like needles and cones but they are angiosperms. The true leaves are brown scales fused in rings on the needle-like branchlets.

Southern blue gum
The flowers of this eucalyptus grow in groups of three inside gumnuts with tops that the flowers push open.

Senegal date palm
The feather-like leaves of the Senegal date palm can grow up to 15 feet (4.5 m) long. The orange fruits hang in large clusters.

Lawson cypress
The pyramid-shaped, evergreen Lawson cypress has small cones with wrinkled scales. Immature cones are bluish green but become brown as they mature.

Bat's wing coral tree
With leaves that look like bat wings and pea-shaped coral pink flowers, the deciduous bat's wing coral tree has thorns on its bark and branches.

World Forests

Almost half of the area that was once forest has disappeared in the last 2,000 years, but forests still cover 30 percent of Earth's land surface. There are six main types of forests, categorized according to the dominant tree species growing in each forest. Climate is the determining factor for tree species—some species can tolerate cold, other species need warmth and large amounts of rain. Latitude determines climate, which is why the different types of forests are in horizontal bands following the lines of latitude.

Remaining forests

Almost 50 percent of remaining forests are in Russia (boreal and coniferous), Brazil (tropical rain forest), and North America (temperate broadleaf and coniferous).

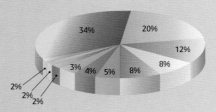

34% 20% 12% 8% 8% 5% 4% 3% 2% 2% 2%

KEY

- Russia
- Brazil
- Canada
- United States
- China
- Australia
- Dem. Rep. Congo
- Indonesia
- Peru
- India
- Others

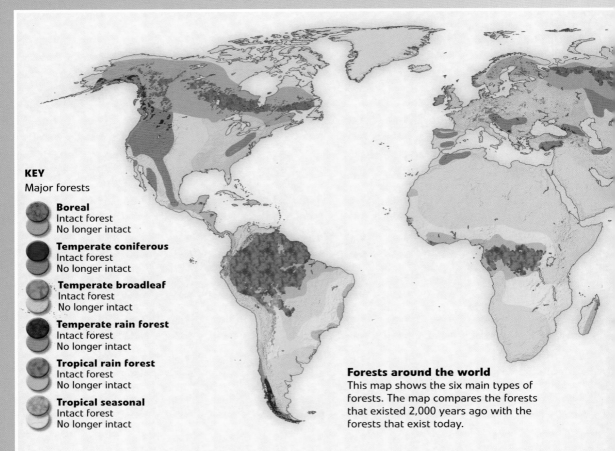

KEY
Major forests

Boreal
Intact forest
No longer intact

Temperate coniferous
Intact forest
No longer intact

Temperate broadleaf
Intact forest
No longer intact

Temperate rain forest
Intact forest
No longer intact

Tropical rain forest
Intact forest
No longer intact

Tropical seasonal
Intact forest
No longer intact

Forests around the world
This map shows the six main types of forests. The map compares the forests that existed 2,000 years ago with the forests that exist today.

Soils and roots

In temperate forests, nutrients lie deep in the soil. Rain forests have poor soil but nutrients come from leaf litter and humus.

Tree roots in temperate forests grow deep into the soil.

Trees in rain forests have shallow roots in the top layers of soil.

CONSERVATION

If we had known in the past what we know now—that forests are a finite resource—more of our forests might have been preserved. Preservation is the best option but conservation is our current solution. Conservation includes increasing public awareness, reforestation, and finding alternative sources for wood.

Reforestation

Reforestation involves growing seedlings of native tree species under nursery conditions then planting them in partially cleared or damaged areas of forest.

Forest plantations

Man-made forests or plantations, where trees are planted and harvested like any other farm crop, now supply some of our needs for timber.

Tree farming

For every Christmas tree bought from this US tree farm, one conifer in a natural forest is saved.

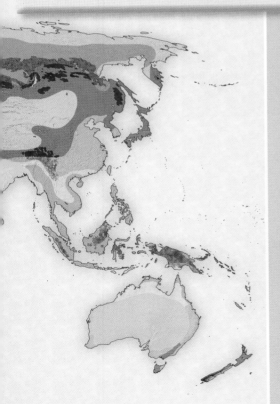

Boreal Forests

The northernmost boreal forests—stretching from Alaska and Canada in the west, through northern Scandinavia to Russia in the east—make up the largest forest area in the world today. In these northern latitudes, winters are very long and very cold; summers are short and wet. Most trees in boreal forests are conifers along with some species of broadleaf trees that can withstand the extreme cold.

THE SAAMI

Approximately 70,000 Saami, thought to be the oldest surviving ethnic group in Europe, herd reindeer in the boreal forests of Norway, Sweden, Finland, and Russia. Their wooden *lavvu*, or huts, are easily dismantled and rebuilt as they move through the forest along with their semi-domesticated reindeer.

Conifers
The life cycle of conifers depends on the winds that sweep through the boreal forest.

Next generation
Some seeds germinate and grow, and the cycle of life begins again.

Pollination
The male cone releases pollen that is blown to a nearby sticky female cone.

Growing seeds
The female cone swells to four times its normal size before releasing the seeds.

Winged seeds
The seeds have wings that allow them to float on the wind to a suitable spot.

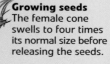

Canada's boreal forests
Almost one-third of the world's boreal forests, also known as taiga, is in Canada. At its broadest, Canada's taiga is more than 620 miles (1,000 km) wide. The forest grew only 5,000 years ago, some time after the last ice age.

Boreal forest animals
Just like tree species, only some animal species are equipped to deal with the cold temperatures of the boreal forest.

Moose
Moose can withstand extreme cold but not heat.

Gray wolf
The wolf's large feet and webbed toes are ideal for walking on snow.

American black bear
Female black bears and cubs hibernate but males are occasionally active in winter.

Porcupine
When climbing trees, a porcupine uses its hind feet and tail quills to hang on.

Temperate Forests

Most of the remaining temperate forests are in the Northern Hemisphere, in a horizontal band between the boreal forests and the Tropic of Cancer. There are three types of temperate forests—broadleaf, coniferous, and the much rarer temperate rain forest. Each type of forest requires different climatic conditions to thrive. Temperature, rainfall, and soil determine which species of trees grow in each forest.

Spring

Coniferous forests

In the coniferous forests of western North America, southern Europe, and Asia, temperatures range from 86°F (30°C) to below zero. Undergrowth is limited: not much can grow in the litter of conifer needles.

Broadleaf forests

The broadleaf forests of North America and Europe contain a wide range of deciduous tree species including beech, oak, elm, willow, maple, hickory, basswood, cottonwood, and magnolia. They also have a rich understory of other plants.

Rain forests

Found in parts of Chile, North America, New Zealand, and Australia, temperate rain forests need high rainfall. In the Northern Hemisphere, conifers are common; in the Southern Hemisphere, tree ferns and broadleaf trees dominate.

Fall

Summer

Animals
The three types of temperate forests offer varied habitats for animals, all of which have a role to play in these ecosystems.

Chipmunk
The North American chipmunk is a voracious feeder on nuts, fruits, and berries.

Fallow deer
The fallow deer is found in Europe's broadleaf forests. Only the male has antlers.

Seasonal changes
A deciduous tree looks very different each season. In broadleaf forests, with their variety of deciduous trees, seasonal changes are even more dramatic—flowers of every color in spring; fruits and nuts in summer; gold, red, and orange leaves in fall; and bare, leafless trees in winter.

Winter

Kakapo
This flightless parrot of New Zealand's rain forest is critically endangered.

Flying squirrel
This squirrel glides between trees in North American temperate forests.

Tropical Forests

O f the two types of tropical forests, rain forests are the more extensive and the better known. These forests, where temperatures range from 68° to 95°F (20–35°C) and annual rainfall exceeds 69 inches (1,750 mm), are found near the equator in South America, Africa, and Southeast Asia. Tropical seasonal forests, found farther away from the equator, have lower rainfall, a long dry season, and contain deciduous trees rather than the evergreen trees of tropical rain forests.

THE YANOMAMI

This tribe lives in the rain forest of Brazil, near the headwaters of the Orinoco River. The Yanomami hunt and gather food from the forest but their staple food is starch-rich plantain (a banana-like fruit) and the termites on plantain leaves.

Strangler fig
This fig is a parasite that grows on a host tree but kills it in the process.

From a fig seed in a high branch of the host tree, a root grows down toward the ground.

When the root reaches the ground, it anchors itself in the soil.

The strangler fig's leaves begin to grow among the leaves of the host tree.

New fig roots grow back up the host tree in a tight lattice.

The roots of the fig strangle the host's trunk, its leaves smother the tree's foliage, and the tree dies.

Making way
When a tree dies in the rain forest, it not only lets the sunlight through to what is normally dark forest floor, but also breaks down to provide nutrients for new trees to grow.

Rain forest animals
Tropical rain forests teem with animal life at every level: dark forest floor, sun-dappled understory, and exposed canopy.

Resplendent quetzal
The quetzal lives in the canopy of Central America's rain forests.

Howler monkey
This noisy monkey scampers from canopy to forest floor.

Red-eyed tree frog
This climbing frog is found at ground and understory levels.

Toucan
The toco toucan nests in tree hollows in the rain forest canopy.

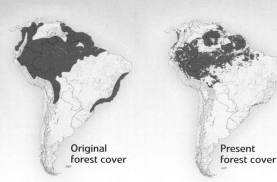

Original
forest cover

Present
forest cover

South American rain forest
The Amazon rain forest, like forests
everywhere, is constantly under threat from
human settlement and the infrastructure that
comes with settlement. An area the size of
New Jersey is cut down every year.

Man-Made Forests

Almost 25 percent of the world's
forests are now man-made. Most
managed forests contain
coniferous trees, which are fast growing.
Every stage—pollination, seedling
growth, planting out, disease
inspection and treatment, and cutting
or felling—is carefully managed. When
some blocks of the forest are felled,
seedlings, saplings, and immature trees
are left to provide future resources.

Managed forests
Each block of the forest
contains trees that were
planted out as seedlings at
the same time, so all of the
trees in that block will be at
the same stage of growth.

Late thinning
Trees are thinned out
after 20–30 years,
allowing more space
for remaining trees.

Planting out
Seedlings are
planted close
together in rows.

Clear felling
A block of
mature trees is
harvested.

European forests

Half of Europe's forests have disappeared, mainly as a result of population growth. Cities, roads, railroads, power stations, and mines now stand where forests once grew.

Original forest cover

Present forest cover

Mature trees
The best of the mature trees grow for 60 years.

Preparing the soil
Needles and roots are mulched to provide nutrients for new seedlings.

Early thinning
Some of the weaker trees are removed and sold.

TREE FARMS

Farm trees are planted in straight lines with spaces between the rows. The spaces allow for mechanized weeding and, when the time comes to harvest the crop, leave motorized power saws enough room to operate.

Totem pole
Carved wooden totems are found in many cultures.

Using Trees

Wood is a versatile material that can be cut to shape, carved, polished, or painted. It is used to construct homes or to make furniture, boats, musical instruments, paper, and pencils. As well as using the timber from trees, we eat tree fruits and nuts, make dyes and fibers from leaves, get rubber or maple syrup from sap, and many of our medicines and antiseptics come from trees—and this treasure trove does not require the tree to be chopped down.

Making a dugout canoe

Coastal and river people around the world have been making wooden boats for centuries. Each culture has its traditional design that best suits local waters.

The log is split lengthwise and shaped to create a flat bottom.

The sides, stern, and bow are shaved to the correct thickness then shaped.

Turned over, the inside is hollowed out.

Filled with hot water, the wood becomes pliable and is expanded by central thwarts.

Bow and stern pieces, often carved or decorated, are fitted.

Medicine from trees

Forest dwellers—and international pharmaceutical companies—know the medicinal qualities of many trees, and more are being discovered.

The anti-malarial drug quinine comes from cinchona tree bark.

Rosy periwinkle is one of many flowers used in cancer drugs.

Computerized cutting
In sawmills, computers calculate how to cut a log to minimize waste and ensure standard lengths of timber.

Grain and color
A thin veneer of attractive wood is often glued on to a less expensive wood.

Mahogany
Wood from the tropical rain forest mahogany tree is used to make guitars and violins.

Oak
Oak is strong and insect resistant so is used mainly in construction.

Ebony
Dark ebony is used to make piano keys and door handles.

Walnut
Walnut is used for wall paneling, gun butts, and in expensive car dashboards.

Cherry
Cherry carves well and is often used in hand-crafted furniture.

Timber houses
In many countries, timber-framed homes are common. Different types of wood are used in the frame, joists, floors, and internal walls.

Tree Facts

There are thousands of fascinating facts about trees because there are so many species and they have such a long history. Some trees grow to amazing heights or live incredibly long lives. Some tree seeds even went to the Moon and back on Apollo 14. Hundreds of these "Moon" trees now grow around the United States.

Long life

Trees are Earth's longest-living organisms. But many die before their time, killed by insects, disease, hurricanes, fires, or wood choppers.

Weevil grubs

Borer

Palm trees

Palm trees have the largest seeds (coconuts), the longest leaves (raffia palm), and are the tallest trees without branches (wax palm). Their barks are fibrous and do not heal when cut.

Palm leaves grow from a single bud.

Spare buds

It is the terminal bud at the end of a tree branch that produces the flowers and leaves. The small lateral buds on the sides of branches are "spares," which grow only if the terminal bud is damaged.

Horse chestnut buds

Fire resistant

Redwood timber buildings resisted the fire that followed the great San Francisco earthquake of 1906, so redwood was used extensively in the rebuilding.

Logging of redwood

Paper

Worldwide, 4 billion trees are converted to wood chips each year, then pulped to produce paper. The average American uses 680 pounds (308 kg) of paper products every year.

Wood chips

Desert trees

To survive the heat and drought of the desert, the quiver tree stores water in its fibrous trunk and thick, fleshy leaves. Pale bark and white branches reflect sunshine and prevent the tree from overheating.

South African quiver tree

Tallest tree
Measured in 2006 at 378 feet (115.2 m) in height, Hyperion, a California coast redwood, is the world's tallest tree.

Oldest living tree
A 4,800-year-old bristlecone pine in California is the world's oldest living tree. A Norway spruce in Sweden has roots that are 9,550 years old but the tree now growing from these roots is much younger.

Glossary

angiosperm
(AN-jee-eh-sperm) A tree that grows flowers and has seeds inside a female carpel. Most trees today are angiosperms, but there are also non-flowering trees called gymnosperms.

anther (AN-thur) The tip of the male stamen, in a flower, that produces pollen.

boreal forests
(BOR-ee-ul FOR-est) The band of forest in the cold far north, up as far as the Arctic. Most of the trees in boreal forests are conifers.

broadleaf (BRAWD-leef) The flat, wide leaf on flowering trees that is often shed in fall.

cambium (KAM-bee-um) A thin layer of cells just beneath a tree's bark, which divide constantly to produce new wood and bark.

canopy (KA-nuh-pee) The branches and leaves on the top layer of a tree that act like a cover for the tree layers below.

carpel (KAHR-pel) The female seed-bearing part of a flower, which contains the ovary and the stigma that collects pollen.

catkin (KAT-kun) A drooping spike of male or female flowers without stalks that grow on some trees, such as willows.

chlorophyll (KLOR-uh-fil) A green substance in the cells of leaves that absorbs energy from sunlight for photosynthesis.

deciduous
(deh-SIH-joo-us) Describes a tree that sheds its leaves in fall and is bare of leaves in winter. The opposite of deciduous is evergreen.

ecosystem
(EE-koh-sis-tem) A community of plants and animals and the physical environment that they share. The ecosystem also includes the soil, water, and inorganic elements in the shared habitat.

embryo (EM-bree-oh) The very early stage of development of any organism. A tree embryo is the tiny plantlet developing inside the fertilized seed before it germinates.

evergreen (EH-ver-green) Describes a tree that does not lose its leaves in fall but has leaves all year round. The opposite of evergreen is deciduous.

germination
(jer-muh-NAY-shun) The stage when a seed sprouts its first stem or root. Germination requires sunlight, moisture, and oxygen.

glucose (GLOO-kohs) A sugar rich in energy that all living things need to grow. Trees make their own glucose in the process of photosynthesis.

growth rings
(GROHTH RINGZ) The rings in a tree trunk that show the yearly growth of the tree. A light-colored ring shows spring growth, a dark ring shows slower, later growth, and the two together show one year's growth.

gymnosperm
(JIM-noh-sperm) A tree that does not flower and produces naked seeds (without ovaries), often inside cones. Conifers, cycads, and ginkgos are all gymnosperms.

heartwood (HART-wood) The oldest and hardest wood at the very center of the tree trunk.

host (HOHST) The tree on which a parasite, such as a strangler fig, lives and feeds.

humus (HUH-mis) A rich mix of soil and partly or wholly decomposed plant material (leaves and wood) lying on the ground.

lateral bud (LAH-tuh-rul BUD) A bud that grows on the side of a twig rather than at the end of the twig. A lateral bud remains dormant unless the bud at the end of the twig is damaged.

minerals (MIN-rulz) Salts absorbed by tree roots from the soil. The minerals come from crushed metals and rocks and include magnesium, iron, potassium, calcium, nitrogen, and phosphorous.

nectar (NEK-tur) A sugary liquid produced by flowers to attract pollinators such as insects and birds.

nutrients (NOO-tree-ents) Substances needed by all living things to grow and thrive. Tree nutrients include minerals from the soil, absorbed by the roots and the glucose or sugars produced in the leaves during photosynthesis.

organism (OR-guh-nih-zum) An individual living thing—plant or animal.

ovary (OH-vuh-ree) The part of a flower that contains the female cell, or ovule. The ovary grows into a fruit after fertilization.

parasite (PER-uh-syt) A plant or fungus that lives and feeds off a host tree, which is damaged or killed by the parasite.

phloem (FLOH-em) Tubes of living cells that transport nutrients around all parts of a tree.

photosynthesis (foh-toh-SIN-thuh-sus) The production of nutrients in the leaves of a tree. Sunlight, minerals, water, and carbon dioxide are all used to produce the sugars or glucose that nourish the tree.

pollen (PAH-lin) Tiny, often yellow, grains produced in flowers or cones that contain the male cells.

pollination (pah-lih-NAY-shun) The transfer of male pollen to a female cell by a pollinator such as an insect, animal, bird, or the wind.

sap (SAP) The liquid containing water, sugars, and minerals that moves up and down the tree trunk to other parts of the tree.

sapling (SAP-ling) A young, immature tree during its first years of growth.

sapwood (SAP-wood) Newly grown wood between the heartwood, at the center of the trunk, and the bark. The sapwood contains the cells that carry water and minerals up the trunk.

spore (SPOR) Tiny one-celled particles that simple plants, such as ferns, use instead of a seed to produce new plants.

stomata (STOH-muh-tuh) Tiny holes in the underside of leaves that open to take in carbon dioxide and to release water and oxygen. The singular is stoma.

taiga (TY-guh) Another name for the mainly coniferous boreal forest of the Far North.

terminal bud (TERM-nul BUD) The most important or dominant bud on the end of a twig that produces the leaves and, sometimes, flowers for next year's growth. Other buds remain dormant and do not develop unless something happens to the terminal bud.

Index

Websites

Due to the changing nature of Internet links, PowerKids Press has developed an online list of websites related to the subject of this book. This site is updated regularly. Please use this link to access the list: www.powerkidslinks.com/disc/forest/